The
Little
Ripple

Balboa Press books may be ordered through booksellers or by contacting:

Balboa Press
A Division of Hay House
1663 Liberty Drive
Bloomington, IN 47403
www.balboapress.com
1 (877) 407-4847

ISBN: 978-1-5043-8795-8 (sc)
ISBN: 978-1-5043-8796-5 (e)

Library of Congress Control Number: 2017914157

Print information available on the last page.

Balboa Press rev. date: 10/31/2017

BALBOA.
PRESS
A DIVISION OF HAY HOUSE

The Little Ripple

DEBRA EMERSON

Illustrated by Grace Talbot

Dedicated to my students who said to me after I recited the children's text that follows, "You should be famous for that!"

Each wave starts as a little ripple
in the water a little tickle
that spreads out
and grows and grows.
Where it stops
we can hardly know.

Each *thought* starts as a little ripple
in the *mind* a little tickle
that spreads out and grows and grows.
Where it stops
we can hardly know.

Each *deed* starts as a little ripple
in the *world* a little tickle
that spreads out
and grows and grows.
Where it stops
we can hardly know.

What we think
and what we do
ripples out and waves;
it's true.

Just think of the good
and do what's kind
and more of the same
is what you'll find.

A Companion to

The Little Ripple

for Adults

including

Activities with Children

On the Birth of This Book

I had caught about the last half of a film on the television depicting ethnic cleansing in Africa. As disturbed as I was about the big troubles over there, I knew how we are also responsible by all our little troubles over here. I wanted to explain this to the children as well as the adults and so this little book.

February 2006

I have taught in the public schools for over 32 years. Many of the disciplinary referrals to the school administrative office have to do with bullying of some kind. Then there was the school assembly where victims of violence were promoting forgiveness and peace. The students were asked to raise their hands if they still had anger toward anyone, and I audibly gasped as I looked around from the back where I was standing. I was shocked that almost every hand in that large high school auditorium went up. As I make it my quest to have nothing between me and anybody else, it became clear that many others do not understand the importance of this mission nor do they have the tools. When we operate from separateness and pain, conflict and confusion follow. Herein are some tools for connection and for peace.

July 2017

A Note to the Adults

It is Independence Day here in America as I revisit this text over a decade later to get this and soon other books ready for publication. I feel like the mother hen finally getting ready to push her hatching brood out of the nest. Considering the idea of independence and freedom, are we ever truly free when the tiny terrorist of our own thinking thrives within? Only when we are free can the world be free too.

In the science of physics, it is known that energy can neither be created nor destroyed though it may change forms. We know that liquid can evaporate and become a gas while when it freezes it becomes a solid, for example. The Butterfly Effect is an additional principle stating that if a butterfly were to flap its wings here the effect would be felt galaxies away. So, collectively we are one energy but many forms; and all that we are and think and say and do affects everyone and everything else.

The violence and cruelty of the ethnic cleansing that inspired this book is not an isolated event for nothing happens in isolation. Each time we personally hold onto emotion or take a position or cling to being right we feed those worldly waves. Also, we have aimed to track down and kill this terrorist or that terrorist. Well, this only eliminates the effect much like unscrewing a light bulb without shutting down the electricity that supplies it. We are the power that runs the world. What kind of a world do we want? Then run that kind of power.

Preface to Activities

These activities are meant to be suggestions and to serve as practical tools for parents, teachers, any adult really, and children alike. Note that these are not activities *for* children but *with* children. We are our children's greatest teacher. They learn from our example. I am reminded of a Ralph Waldo Emerson quote: "What you are speaks so loudly over your head that I cannot hear what you say."

Children swim in our psyche and encounter pieces of our past pain hidden there that we have submerged long ago and cannot see, our shadow side. "Shadow" not because it is dark as in ominous or evil but "shadow" because it is not in the light so we are not aware it is lurking there. Our children may mirror our unresolved past, and the family therefore can become the main unit for transformation and peace in the present. I was thirty years old when I first started to become conscious of my shadow side. What if through the process of working on our own enlightenment we give the children tools to navigate emotional waters as they arise? They can go into adulthood with experience but without the stored pain, without needing to unwind thirty years of unknowing…as in my case, without the ripples that feed the negative waves on the planet. I see a new heaven and a new earth on the horizon.

Suggested resources at this time? There is Jean Liedloff's book *The Continuum Concept: In Search of Happiness Lost* about her observations of child-rearing and society in the Yequana tribe in South America. Then there's the work of Byron Katie and, in particular, see her book *Loving What Is*. EFT or Emotional Freedom Technique is also key, and Nick Ortner's work in this area is top notch so see his book *The Tapping Solution*. Other recommendations are Joseph Chilton Pearce's *Magical Child*, Barry Long's *Raising Children in Love, Justice*, and *Truth*, and the work of Dr. Shefali Tsabary such as *The Conscious Parent*, recently recommended to me by a friend. I have started listening to her talks on YouTube and so much is available there, and let me not forget Marshall Rosenberg and *Nonviolent Communication: A Language of Life*. I have also been listening to him on YouTube. I love YouTube. We tend to have such busy lives but I find time by bringing my laptop into the bedroom while I fold and put away the laundry or into the kitchen while I prepare dinner, and I have a listen. It's easy to pause a talk if there is an interruption. I keep my cellphone or a notebook nearby in case I want to record a thought or jot something down. Perhaps this will work for you too or you may find other windows of opportunity such as listening to audio books when taking trips in the car.

Since the activities that follow are meant to be integrated simply into your everyday life, you could choose one a week to work with daily until it becomes habit and so on. Be light and easy as you step lightly into more and more light.

Activities with Children

Watch your thoughts. Most of us are entirely unconscious of what we are allowing to run our minds and in turn run our world including the world at large. Like "musack" in the elevator, we tune it out and don't really notice it but it is there and colors our lives nevertheless. To help watch the thoughts, wear an unusual piece of jewelry or move a ring you always wear to a different finger or hand. Or, make "thought buster bracelets." Feel free to be creative. Every time you notice that jewelry, like a string tied around your finger, it is a reminder to stop and observe: what am I thinking? First, the stopping breaks the mental momentum. Then, becoming aware of what thoughts are running helps you begin to become aware of how they are feeding the patterns that are creating the circumstances of your life.

Warning: Judge not these thoughts...however emotional or negative. They are not necessarily logical....nor is ethnic cleansing. They may not even be particularly personal. Remember the ripple effect: the waves can flow out of us but can also flow into us. Finally, avoid analyzing. This just feeds the mind more. Simply observe without judgment. In time the emotional thinking will diminish. Practical thought is really the only necessity of the mind. As an exercise, you can ask yourself, "Is there any practical action I can take?" If not, allow the simple act of observation to still the rising mental and emotional momentum.

Parent the inner child. How would you speak to your child if he or she came to you in pain? Speak to your pain the same way and surround it with understanding and love. In turn, you can teach your child to give his or her emotion understanding, compassion, and love too.

Take timeouts. To minimize emotional reactions and maximize constructive interactions, take time away from a charged situation. You may see the wounded child acting out in anyone treating you in a less than kind way. Take a step back from reacting to allow things to simmer down and gain perspective.

Transform darkness into light. Adopt Byron Katie's inquiry and turn-around technique or EFT for yourself. These are my go-to tools. See *www.thework.com* and *www.thetappingsolution.com*. Then you can guide your children to use either when emotion arises, or both as I sometimes find it helpful to cross train, so to speak. Tap with them, or do the inquiry and turn-around with them. Working with the children will be enlightening for you too. My friend told me of a child who said to her yelling mother, "You maybe should tap now, Mommy."

Come to your senses. When emotional, we get lost in our heads and lose connection to our bodies. Get physical. Shake, rattle, and roll. Shake your hands and feet out. Rattle your arms and legs about. Roll around the floor. Dance. Stomp about and get grounded. Shake or walk out the sad, scared, or mad.

Be where your body is and breathe. A client called hysterical and couldn't breathe. "Breathe out, breathe out, breathe out," I kept telling her until her natural in-breaths followed. Next I had her squeeze all the muscles of her body as tight as she could and hold it as long as she could. And again. And a third time. Then she was in her body once more and calm. She briefly told me what had caused the hysteria which when in her body again was no longer a cause of panic. We looked at the facts, outlined possible actions, and she chose one. It was done. If all throughout the day we practice being in our senses or just doing random muscle contractions, we ground and it's easier for us to maintain our center when we feel the emotions start to rise.

Be selective about the media to which your child is exposed. This is especially important during the early foundational years. No matter the age, words and images convey a message and an energy. Be aware that it is one you feel should be fed in your life and on the planet. See *The Hidden Messages from Water* book and *Messages from Water* video by Masaru Emoto. His experiments are really interesting and important! Read and watch with your children. This experience will help involve them in the media selection process as well as open up some other doors.

Keep gratitude journals or blessings books. They can be just drawings with a word or a sentence you write for your child or more involved books depending on their ages. Even my grandmother at age 84 was helped by this technique. Energy flows where attention goes. When we are grateful and focused on the good, it brings more of the same.

When an emotional situation arises, use this formula:

1. Separate the facts from the feelings.
2. Look at the facts without blaming, complaining, or judging which is more mind-stuff that keeps us emotional. *Remember that we are the cause, the little ripple. The situation, the wave, is just the effect.*
3. Look at the possible actions.
4. Take the action that looks like "the biggest yes."
5. Smile and acknowledge the good, in your body as a sensation and in your life; you can simply give thanks.

"Action always purifies," Barry Long would say and he meant that as we do the previous process we weaken the emotional tyrant by not giving him or her free reign until eventually he or she no longer arises. As we become such people of action, we are less victims of *reaction*. My friend's ten year old was balking about going to a hockey game and his father threw up his hands. I used this technique with the child as a series of questions in just a couple of minutes, and he was happy to be heading off to play hockey. His father was happy too.

Apply the THINK acronym. Before speaking or acting, THINK: Is it True? Helpful? Inspiring? Necessary? Kind?

Get involved in a community service project. Not only can this help the child develop compassion and see that the world is bigger than his or her own backyard, but it is also great family time too. Connection to family and community breeds positive self-esteem.

Tame excitement. Know this is differentiated from passion or joy. Violence, what inspired this book, is a form of excitement, frenzied emotion. Look at where you or your children are overly excited about anything. Pause until that frenzy can be grounded. Feel the sensation in the hands or the feet, and then you can go forward with the activity.

Continually feel the good as a sensation in your body, and see all that is good around you as a reflection of that. Remember the goodness does not originate in the external forms as the electricity does not originate in the light bulbs. Goodness is the power of love within each and the power that connects all. Only those feeling powerless may feel the need to control to gain power over another. Keep it simple for yourself and for the children. Keep connected. Keep bringing the focus back to the good which can break the habit of the negative. If we surround negativity with good—which is the life, love, and one energy that is—it trans-forms. "All emotion is just love that has not been acknowledged," said Barry Long. Of course, there is only one energy anyway. We have created the form of the negativity and we can therefore un-create it. What each one of us does for ourselves, we do for our children, our families, our friends, our communities, and the entire planet.

Acknowledgements

Thanks go particularly to the influence of spiritual teacher Barry Long, to the practical wisdom of Fiona Whitmore, to the editing advice of Diane Miazga, and to the artistic and technical support of Patty Valens.

CPSIA information can be obtained
at www.ICGtesting.com
Printed in the USA
BVHW020227270919
559612BV00016B/216/P